Katie Powers

FUNNY TRIVIA FOR SENIORS

CHAPTERS LIST

THANK YOU!

As the scribbler behind this hilariously enlightening trivia book for the young at heart, I want to tip my hat and offer a giant, confetti-filled **THANK YOU** for letting us sneak into your homes and maybe even your hearts.

If our book cracked you up, made you scratch your head, or even had you reminiscing about the good ol' days, consider leaving us a review on Amazon. Just a few words from you can boost our spirits, spread the joy, and maybe convince others that it's never too late to have a good laugh.

Leaving a review is easier than explaining to your grandkids what a rotary phone is. But your feedback? It's gold to us, more precious than that "antique" you keep hidden from the kids.

Got something to say, a bone to pick, or just want to share a joke? We're all ears! Drop us a line or send a carrier pigeon. We love hearing from our band of merry trivia masters.

With a wink and a smile,

Katie Powers

Contact Us Before We Forget How to Use Technology:

Email: hello@bluedunes.org and Yes, We Do Check It

Hitch a Ride to the 1950s: Where the Cars Were Almost as Big as the Hair!

Welcome to the 1950s: a decade where skirts got shorter, cars got bigger, and TVs made their grand entrance into living rooms worldwide! Imagine rock 'n' roll blasting from jukeboxes, teens doing the twist, and families gathering around to watch the first-ever color broadcast. This was a time when sending a man to space was just a twinkle in science's eye, and the word "computer" would likely conjure images of a very diligent person with a calculator rather than a sleek, digital device.

In the midst of Cold War tensions, the world also found ways to let loose. Elvis Presley's hips caused more uproar than some political debates, and the race to the moon seemed like humanity's most ambitious bet yet.
Fast food became a thing, with diners and drive-ins revolutionizing the way we eat—because who wouldn't want their milkshake delivered by someone on roller skates?

So, buckle up (or should we say, strap on your saddle shoes?) for a trip back to the 1950s. It was a decade of contrasts, where traditional values met the pioneering edge of the new age, and poodle skirts weren't just fashion statements —they were rebellion incarnate.

Let's dive into the atomic age, where every day felt a bit like living in a sci-fi novel, but with better music and way cooler cars. Welcome to the fabulous '50s, where the future was so bright, you had to wear shades—preferably at the drive-in movie theater.

1. What was the "cool" new pet for kids in the 1950s, which required virtually no care but also didn't do much?
- A) The Pet Rock
- B) Sea-Monkeys
- C) Ant Farms
- D) Invisible Dogs

2. What was a teenager's best defense against cooties in the 1950s?
- A) Bubble gum
- B) Hula Hoop
- C) Duct tape
- D) Cootie catcher

3. In the 1950s, what was considered the ultimate status symbol for suburban families?
- A) A color TV
- B) A pet rock
- C) A two-car garage
- D) A pink flamingo for the yard

4. What was the 1950s equivalent of a home theater system?

- A) A radio the size of a refrigerator
- B) A drive-in movie theater
- C) A cardboard box with a hole cut out for the screen
- D) A book and a vivid imagination

5. What 1950s health fad promised to jiggle away fat without lifting a finger?

- A) The Hula Hoop Diet.
- B) The Jell-O Wiggle Workout
- C) The Vibrating Belt Machine
- D) The Twist Challenge

6. In the 1950s, what was the best way to predict the weather?

- A) A weather rock
- B) Licking your finger and sticking it in the air
- C) Asking the neighbor
- D) Watching the clouds while lying on the grass

7. What was the must-have hairstyle for women in the 1950s that required copious amounts of hairspray to maintain its gravity-defying shape?

- A) The Straight and Narrow
- B) The Beehive
- C) The Poodle Cut
- D) The Bouffant

8. Which of these iconic 1950s TV shows featured a character from another planet long before sci-fi took over our screens?

- A) "I Love Lucy"
- B) "Leave It to Beaver"
- C) "My Favorite Martian"
- D) "The Honeymooners"

9. In the 1950s, which product was advertised as a "miracle" for women, claiming to offer an instant hourglass figure?

- A) Spandex
- B) The Magic Girdle
- C) Polyester Pants
- D) Poodle Skirts

10. Which of the following items became a controversial fashion icon in the 1950s, leading to debates in schools across America?

- A) Leather Jackets
- B) Blue Jeans
- C) Saddle Shoes
- D) Cardigan Sweaters

11. What was considered the height of luxury in home entertainment during the 1950s, a status symbol in many living rooms?

- A) The Color Television
- B) The Hi-Fi Record Player
- C) The Reclining Armchair
- D) The Radio-Phonograph Combo

12. Which of these 1950s innovations was thought to potentially revolutionize personal transportation, yet never quite took off?

- A) The Flying Car
- B) The Hoverboard
- C) The Electric Scooter
- D) The Jetpack

13. In the 1950s, which of these was a popular diet trend that promised weight loss without cutting out the steaks and shakes?
- A) The Grapefruit Diet
- B) The Cabbage Soup Diet
- C) The High-Protein, Low-Carb Diet
- D) The Tapeworm Diet

14. What did teenagers in the 1950s call the act of driving around aimlessly, a favorite weekend activity?
- A) Wheel Wobbling
- B) Drag Racing
- C) Cruising
- D) Joy Riding

15. What 1950s dance move shocked the world with its simplicity and has everyone literally just standing still?
- A) The Twist
- B) The Moonwalk
- C) The Freeze
- D) The Hula Hoop

16. In the 1950s, which household item was considered so cutting-edge, that people would gather around to watch it work?

- A) The Automatic Dishwasher
- B) The Electric Can Opener
- C) The Color Television
- D) The Vacuum Cleaner

17. Which 1950s food innovation was originally intended for astronauts but ended up in every American kid's lunchbox instead?

- A) Tang
- B) Freeze-Dried Ice Cream
- C) Instant Mashed Potatoes
- D) Peanut Butter & Jelly in a Can

18. What was the '50s teen's answer to a mobile phone, allowing them to stretch away from eavesdropping parents while chatting with friends?

- A) The Telephone Booth
- B) The 20-Foot Phone Cord
- C) The Walkie-Talkie
- D) The Two-Can Telephone

19. Which of these was a groundbreaking '50s fashion trend that allowed teens to rebel without saying a word?
- A) Turtlenecks
- B) Poodle Skirts
- C) T-shirts and Jeans
- D) Leather Jackets

20. What 1950s 'technology' promised to teach languages overnight, making dreams of effortless learning a pillow away?
- A) Sleep Learning Records
- B) The Language Learning Radio
- C) The Subliminal Tape Recorder
- D) The Dream Translator

21. In the 1950s, which innovation in movie theaters was supposed to replicate the experience of being there, long before 3D glasses?
- A) Smell-O-Vision
- B) The Drive-In Theater
- C) Seat Vibrators
- D) Surround Sound

22. What was the quintessential '50s party food, combining exotic pineapple with ordinary ham, showcasing America's post-war fascination with canned food?
- A) Pineapple Ham Delight
- B) The SPAM Surprise
- C) Hawaiian Pizza
- D) Ham and Pineapple Skewers

23. Which household chore in the 1950s became slightly more bearable with the invention of this 'futuristic' appliance?
- A) The Robotic Vacuum
- B) The Electric Iron
- C) The Dishwasher
- D) The Self-Cleaning Oven

24. Which of these was an essential fashion accessory in the '50s, signaling a mix of rebellion and style, especially among the younger crowd?
- A) The Polka Dot Bandana
- B) Cat-Eye Glasses
- C) The Leather Belt
- D) White Socks and Loafers

25. What '50s innovation turned backyard gatherings into a fiery spectacle, introducing Americans to the art of grilling?

- A) The Charcoal Grill
- B) The Gas Grill
- C) The Portable Stove
- D) The Fire Pit

26. Which beloved '50s TV character was known for their zany antics and a love of chocolate, often leading to hilariously sticky situations?

- A) Ralph Kramden
- B) Lucy Ricardo
- C) Beaver Cleaver
- D) Ed Norton

27. In the 1950s, what term was coined to describe the phenomenon of watching too much TV, a concern that seems almost quaint today?

- A) Square Eyes
- B) The Boob Tube Obsession
- C) Televisionitis
- D) The Lazy Eye Epidemic

28. In the 1950s, this automotive feature was introduced as a luxury, symbolizing the ultimate in driving comfort and innovation. What was it?

- A) Power Steering
- B) Seat Belts
- C) Air Conditioning
- D) Tail Fins

29. Which of the following 1950s TV characters was known for their space adventures, long before the actual moon landing?

- A) Captain Video
- B) Flash Gordon
- C) Buck Rogers
- D) Tommy Tomorrow

30. This 1950s fashion trend for men caused quite a stir for its bold attempt to add color and flair to the male wardrobe. What was it?

- A) Argyle Socks
- B) Zoot Suits
- C) Hawaiian Shirts
- D) Pink Shirts

31. What was the name of the first animated feature film to be released in widescreen Cinemascope in the 1950s, signaling a new era for animated storytelling?

- A) Cinderella
- B) Peter Pan
- C) Lady and the Tramp
- D) Sleeping Beauty

32. The 1950s saw the introduction of this toy, which was originally intended as a therapeutic tool for adults before becoming a worldwide child's plaything. What is it?

- A) The Slinky
- B) Play-Doh
- C) The Yo-Yo
- D) LEGO Bricks

33. This iconic 1950s movie monster was a metaphor for public fears about nuclear war and radiation. Who was it?

- A) Godzilla
- B) King Kong
- C) The Creature from the Black Lagoon
- D) The Blob

34. In the late 1950s, a novel culinary invention combined a canned meat product with a certain type of dough, creating a dish that some adore and others deplore. What was it?
- A) SPAM and Beans
- B) SPAMburger Hamburger
- C) SPAM Sushi
- D) SPAM Pizza

35. This controversial dietary product of the 1950s promised weight loss by substituting meals with a liquid solution, predating modern meal replacement shakes. What was it called?
- A) Metrecal
- B) SlimFast
- C) Diet Delight
- D) Liquid Lunch

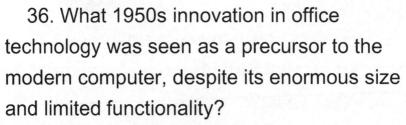

36. What 1950s innovation in office technology was seen as a precursor to the modern computer, despite its enormous size and limited functionality?
- A) The Electric Typewriter
- B) The Fax Machine
- C) The Mainframe Computer
- D) The Photocopier

37. This 1950s invention allowed people to 'see' who was calling them on the phone before answering, a novelty at the time. What was it?

- A) The Caller ID
- B) The Picture Phone
- C) The Video Phone
- D) The Pre-Call Viewer

38. What was the name of the first credit card, introduced in the 1950s, which revolutionized the way people shopped and managed personal finance?

- A) MasterCharge
- B) Diners Club Card
- C) American Express
- D) Visa

39. In the 1950s, this experimental community promised futuristic living with homes equipped with push-button conveniences from floor to ceiling. What was it called?

- A) Epcot
- B) Tomorrowland
- C) Futurama
- D) Levittown

40. Which 1950s TV show used a puppet to address complex issues of the day, becoming an unlikely source of satire and commentary?
- A) The Ed Sullivan Show
- B) Kukla, Fran and Ollie
- C) The Howdy Doody Show
- D) Time for Beany

41. This 1950s innovation was intended to streamline shopping, allowing customers to select groceries without leaving their cars. What was it called?
- A) Drive-Thru Grocery Store
- B) Carhop Supermarket
- C) Automart
- D) Shop-o-Matic

42. In the 1950s, what novel accessory was marketed to pet owners, promising to translate dog barks into human language?
- A) Bark Translator
- B) Canine Communicator
- C) The Woof-O-Matic
- D) Fido's Speaker

43. Which of these was a genuine 1950s board game that simulated the thrilling life of a suburban homeowner?

- A) Dream House
- B) Mortgage Mania
- C) The Game of Life
- D) Home Sweet Home

44. This 1950s fashion trend for men dared to break the monotony of the suit and tie by introducing what exotic garment?

- A) The Hawaiian Shirt
- B) The Leisure Suit
- C) The Smoking Jacket
- D) Bermuda Shorts

45. In the 1950s, a unique beauty contest judged contestants in a rather unconventional way. What was it based on?

- A) Hairstyle Originality
- B) Ankle Beauty
- C) Best Dressed Pet
- D) Telephone Voice Charm

46. What was the name of the first fully enclosed shopping mall in the United States, heralding a new era of consumer culture in the 1950s?

- A) Southdale Center
- B) King of Prussia Mall
- C) Mall of America
- D) The Galleria

47. The 1950s saw the creation of this peculiar musical instrument, which produced sound electronically and was played without being touched. What is it?

- A) The Moog Synthesizer
- B) The Theremin
- C) Electric Organ
- D) Keytar

48. What 1950s fashion accessory was a must-have for every teen girl, serving both as a fashion statement and a symbol of youth culture?

- A) The Poodle Skirt
- B) Bobby Socks
- C) Charm Bracelets
- D) Saddle Shoes

49. In the 1950s, this "futuristic" food product was introduced, offering a new and convenient way to make sandwiches without the hassle of slicing. What was it?
- A) Sliced Bread
- B) Spray Cheese
- C) Pre-Sliced Cheese
- D) Canned Bread

50. This 1950s invention promised to revolutionize personal grooming by eliminating the need for water. What was it?
- A) Dry Shampoo
- B) The Electric Razor
- C) Disposable Razors
- D) The Hair Dryer

51. What unique form of entertainment, combining art and technology, became a mesmerizing attraction at fairs and exhibitions in the 1950s?
- A) 3D Movies
- B) Laser Light Shows
- C) The Kaleidoscope Booth
- D) The Color Organ

52. In an attempt to add novelty to the dining experience, this 1950s invention allowed diners to cook their own food at the table. What was it?

- A) The Hibachi Grill
- B) The Toaster Oven
- C) The Tabletop Grill
- D) The Raclette Grill

53. In the 1950s, this type of restaurant began to rise in popularity, characterized by its carhops and a menu focused on burgers and milkshakes. What was it?

- A) The Diner
- B) The Drive-In
- C) The Fast Food Joint
- D) The Coffee Shop

54. What 1950s toy became an overnight sensation, allowing kids and adults alike to create glowing art with the flick of a wrist?

- A) The Magic Marker
- B) The Lite-Brite
- C) The Glow Worm
- D) The Hula Hoop

55. What quirky 1950s TV show featured a family of puppets living in a magical forest, captivating children and adults alike?

- A) The Magic Roundabout
- B) The Adventures of Gumby
- C) The Enchanted Wood
- D) The Friendly Giant

56. In the 1950s, this became the unexpected fashion craze among teenagers, originally used for a much more practical purpose. What was it?

- A) Bandanas
- B) Military Surplus Jackets
- C) Saddle Shoes
- D) Dog Tags

57. This 1950s "technology" was advertised to housewives as a way to complete household chores with minimal effort, thanks to "atomic" advancements. What was it?

- A) The Atomic Vacuum
- B) The Nuclear-Powered Oven
- C) The Radiation Dishwasher
- D) The Robotic Maid

58.In the 1950s, this piece of furniture became a symbol of suburban living, designed to showcase one particular household item. What was it?

- A) The Sofa Bed
- B) The Television Stand
- C) The Recliner Chair
- D) The Coffee Table

59. This 1950s health craze, promoted by a doctor, involved wearing shoes with uneven soles to improve posture. What was it called?

- A) Balance Boots
- B) Wobble Shoes
- C) The Palmer Method
- D) Earth Shoes

60. This dietary trend of the 1950s, involving a certain grapefruit at every meal, promised weight loss miracles. What was it famously called?

- A) The Citrus Slim-Down
- B) The Hollywood Diet
- C) The Grapefruit Miracle
- D) The Florida Diet

HILARIOUS FACTS OF THE 50s

The Great Canadian Spaghetti Harvest: In 1957, the BBC pulled off one of the most famous April Fools' Day hoaxes of all time. They broadcast a segment about Swiss farmers enjoying a bumper spaghetti crop, showing families plucking strands of spaghetti from trees. Viewers were so intrigued (and some quite fooled) by the concept of spaghetti growing on trees that many called in asking how they could grow their own spaghetti trees. The BBC's advice? "Place a sprig of spaghetti in a tin of tomato sauce and hope for the best."

HILARIOUS FACTS OF THE 50s

Flying Saucer Housekeeping:

The 1950s were all about the space race and futuristic living. So much so, that a company in 1956 actually tried to sell a flying saucer-shaped home that was supposed to be the answer to housekeeping woes—claiming it was designed for easy cleaning. The pitch was that the entire house could be hosed down, with water draining through strategically placed holes in the floor. Imagine the scene: A homeowner in a futuristic flying saucer home, blasting away dirt with a hose, only to realize they've also watered all their indoor plants, the dog, and maybe a visiting neighbor.

HILARIOUS FACTS OF THE 50s

The CIA's Acoustic Kitty Project: In the 1950s, amidst Cold War paranoia, the CIA launched one of its most bizarre espionage experiments: the Acoustic Kitty Project. The idea was to use cats, equipped with tiny bugging devices, to spy on Soviet embassies and officials. The theory was that cats are naturally inconspicuous and could wander in and out of enemy territories undetected. However, after spending millions of dollars and years of training, the project was deemed a failure when the first cat was released near a Soviet compound and immediately ran into traffic. It turns out you can equip a cat with the most sophisticated spying technology, but you can't make it forget its cat instincts.

Groovy Times and Moon Landings: A Hippy-Dippy Trip Through the Swinging '60s

Ah, the 1960s: a decade where the music was revolutionary, the fashion was far-out, and everyone was trying to make "peace" not "war"—except when battling over the last slice of colorfully iced cake at a Beatles-themed birthday party. It was a time when astronauts took one small step for man and one giant leap for mankind, all while folks back on Earth were taking their own giant leaps into inflatable furniture.

The '60s were like the wild younger sibling of the decades, sporting tie-dye shirts, flaunting bell-bottoms, and letting their hair grow long and free—much to the dismay of the neighborhood association. This was the era that gave us Woodstock, where the only thing higher than the music on the charts was, well, the audience. And let's not forget the television, which brought families together with shows that were as much about space and spies as they were about family and morality. **30**

Cars got sleeker, skirts got shorter, and the world seemed to spin just a bit faster as mankind raced to the moon, fought for civil rights, and tuned in to watch a man walk on the moon live on TV. The '60s: when coffeehouses were the Twitter of the day, every conversation was a potential revolution, and if you remember it all too clearly, you probably weren't there. Welcome to the decade where everything changed, including the way we see the world—and beyond.

1. What was the unofficial uniform of the 1960s counterculture, signaling you were cool, hip, and possibly owned a lava lamp?

- A) The Business Suit
- B) Tie-Dye Shirts
- C) The Pilgrim Dress
- D) Knight Armor

2. In the 1960s, which band was more famous than "cheese" (according to John Lennon, at least)?

- A) The Rolling Scones
- B) The Beatles
- C) Led Zeppel-in-a-Tea-Cup
- D) The Who's-on-First

3. What did people in the 1960s blame for making their children rebellious, much like video games are blamed today?

- A) The Wheel
- B) Rock 'n' Roll
- C) Electric Can Openers
- D) The Pet Rock

4. Which 1960s TV show predicted a future with talking computers, yet missed predicting the need for more than one bathroom on a spaceship?

- A) Lost in Space
- B) Doctor What?
- C) Star Trek
- D) The Twilight Zone

5. What was considered the most "far out" mode of transportation in the 1960s, despite never really taking off?

- A) The Hoverboard
- B) The Flying Car
- C) The Skateboard
- D) The Unicycle

6. Which 1960s food innovation promised a full meal in a pill, ideal for those too busy doing the twist to sit down for dinner?

- A) The TV Dinner
- B) Space Food Sticks
- C) The Meal Pill
- D) Tang

7. In the '60s, this was a common way to say "hello" without speaking. Hint: It involved your fingers and a lot of peace.

- A) The Handshake
- B) The Peace Sign
- C) Thumbs Up
- D) Waving

8. Which of these was a real 1960s fad that involved staring at a poster until you saw a "hidden" 3D image?
- A) Magic Eye Posters
- B) Psychedelic Posters
- C) X-Ray Specs Ads
- D) Lava Lamps

9. In the 1960s, what was the revolutionary kitchen appliance that promised to make slicing bread obsolete, stirring up quite the "spread"?
- A) The Electric Knife
- B) The Bread Machine
- C) Pre-Sliced Bread
- D) The Toaster

10. Which 1960s dance move convinced millions that they could actually dance just by shuffling their feet and swinging their arms?
- A) The Moonwalk
- B) The Robot
- C) The Twist
- D) The Mashed Potato

11. What was the go-to 1960s method for making a small room seem larger, without actually knocking down walls?
- A) Mirrors Everywhere
- B) Shag Carpets
- C) Lava Lamps in Every Corner
- D) Psychedelic Wallpaper

12. In the 1960s, which fashion accessory was an absolute must-have for spy enthusiasts and wannabe secret agents?
- A) The Bowler Hat
- B) X-Ray Glasses
- C) The Trench Coat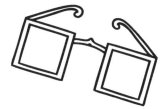
- D) The Shoe Phone

13. Which of these was an actual fashion statement in the 1960s, known for its "electrifying" aesthetic?
- A) Battery-Operated Hats
- B) Glow-in-the-Dark Ties
- C) Solar-Powered Sunglasses
- D) Neon Bell-Bottoms

14. In the '60s, this "space-age" material was all the rage, used for everything from furniture to fashion. What was it?
- A) Aluminum Foil
- B) Spandex
- C) Plastic
- D) Moon Rock

15. What 1960s dance move involved pretending you were drying your back with a towel, and why didn't anyone question this?
- A) The Shimmy
- B) The Twist
- C) The Swim
- D) The Shake

16. Which 1960s invention was supposed to revolutionize personal communication but ended up being used mostly to order pizza?
- A) The Mobile Phone
- B) The Fax Machine
- C) The Answering Machine
- D) The Pager

17. In the 1960s, what was the ultimate "do-it-yourself" project for kids, potentially leading to life-long trauma from splinters?
- A) Building a Treehouse
- B) Making Your Own Yo-Yo
- C) Constructing a Soapbox Derby Car
- D) Knitting Your Own Socks

18. Which '60s TV family had a pet dinosaur, proving once and for all that pet insurance policies were much more flexible back then?
- A) The Jetsons
- B) The Flintstones
- C) The Addams Family
- D) The Munsters

19. What 1960s vehicle became synonymous with road trips and freedom, despite its tendency to be a bit of a gas guzzler?
- A) The Station Wagon
- B) The Mini Cooper
- C) The Volkswagen Bus
- D) The Mustang

20. What 1960s "technology" promised to teach you a new language while you slept, presumably by osmosis?
- A) Sleep Tapes
- B) The Radio
- C) Language Pillows
- D) Subliminal Records

21. Which of these was an actual product of the 1960s, designed to help homeowners take part in the space race from their backyards?
- A) DIY Rocket Kits
- B) Personal Telescopes
- C) Moon Dust Fertilizer
- D) Astronaut Training Manuals

22.What 1960s fashion accessory became notorious for its potential to double as a makeshift weapon?
- A) Peace Sign Necklaces
- B) Go-Go Boots
- C) Beaded Curtains
- D) Pointy Bra

23. In the 1960s, this new food sensation hit the stores, baffling many with its longevity and shelf stability. What was it?
- A) Instant Mashed Potatoes
- B) Tang
- C) Spam
- D) Twinkies

24. What became an unexpected kitchen gadget hit in the 1960s, primarily because it could puree, liquefy, and even sometimes destroy spoons by accident?
- A) The Electric Can Opener
- B) The Blender
- C) The Microwave Oven
- D) The Dishwasher

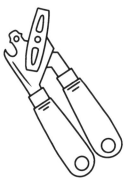

25. Which 1960s fashion trend involved wearing pants so tight, that you needed a friend and possibly a can of grease to help you get into them?

- A) Bell-bottoms
- B) Miniskirts
- C) Poodle skirts
- D) Drainpipe trousers

26. What 1960s "high-tech" toy allowed kids to draw in the air, hinting at a future where 3D printing pens might be a thing?

- A) The Magic Marker
- B) Spirograph
- C) Etch A Sketch
- D) Lite-Brite

27. Which iconic 1960s music festival is best remembered for peace, love, and mud?

- A) Woodstock
- B) Monterey Pop Festival
- C) Altamont Free Concert
- D) Isle of Wight Festival

28. In the 1960s, which "futuristic" home feature turned out to be less about convenience and more about turning a quick snack into a waiting game?
- A) The Instant Hot Water Tap
- B) The Self-Cleaning Oven
- C) The Push-Button Telephone
- D) The Electric Can Opener

29. This 1960s beverage was marketed as a "space-age drink" because astronauts took it to space, making every sip a small step for man.
- A) Tang
- B) Kool-Aid
- C) Coca-Cola
- D) Pepsi

30. Which 1960s animated TV show predicted a future filled with flying cars and robot maids, yet missed the mark on digital spam?
- A) The Jetsons
- B) The Flintstones
- C) Futurama
- D) Astro Boy

31. Which of these was a real 1960s beverage that tried to combine dinner and dessert in one convenient, questionable bottle?
- A) Meatshake
- B) Dinner Cola
- C) Bacon Soda
- D) Vegetable Smoothie

32. What 1960s "innovation" in education involved students learning from recordings instead of teachers, foreshadowing online courses?
- A) The Teaching Machine
- B) Educational Radio
- C) Language Labs
- D) Filmstrip Fridays

33. In the 1960s, what was touted as the "furniture of the future," only to have its popularity deflate like a punctured balloon?
- A) The Inflatable Chair
- B) The Bean Bag
- C) The Futon
- D) The Recliner

34. What 1960s phenomenon led to millions of people staring at black and white swirling patterns, claiming it was "totally far out, man"?

- A) Hypnosis LP Records
- B) The Lava Lamp's Early Prototype
- C) Optical Art (Op Art)
- D) Early Television Static

35. In the 1960s, this gadget promised to wake you up gently to the smell of freshly brewed coffee. What was its major drawback?

- A) The risk of bedside flooding
- B) Coffee grounds in your bed
- C) It was just a dream
- D) Alarmingly high caffeine levels by your pillow

36. What was the "must-have" 1960s gadget for young spies and detectives, aside from a keen sense of skepticism?

- A) X-Ray Glasses
- B) The Invisible Ink Pen
- C) The Decoder Ring
- D) A Trench Coat

43

37. In the 1960s, this home accessory became a symbol of sophistication and mystery, mostly because no one really knew how it worked.

- A) The Lava Lamp
- B) The Recliner Chair
- C) The Rotary Phone
- D) The Fondue Set

38. Which of the following was an actual 1960s children's toy that could also double as a makeshift weapon in sibling rivalries?

- A) The Easy-Bake Oven
- B) Lincoln Logs
- C) The Wham-O Super Ball
- D) Silly Putty

39. What 1960s fashion trend proved that pants could indeed get tighter and colors could always get louder?

- A) Bell-bottoms
- B) Tie-dye shirts
- C) Mini skirts
- D) Go-go boots

40. Which 1960s toy promised to be "fun for a girl and a boy," unless you stepped on it barefoot in the dark?
- A) Barbie and Ken Dolls
- B) The Slinky
- C) LEGO Bricks
- D) Etch A Sketch

41. What was the pinnacle of home entertainment technology in the 1960s, making "slideshow night" an event to remember (or forget)?
- A) The Color Television
- B) The Home Movie Projector
- C) The Slide Projector
- D) The Portable Radio

42. In the 1960s, which board game did families play that was basically about real estate mogul dreams and crushing your opponents into bankruptcy?
- A) Life
- B) Clue
- C) Scrabble
- D) Monopoly

43. Which of these was an actual book turned into a cult classic film in the '60s, featuring carnivorous plants and a very unusual flower shop?

- A) "The Day of the Triffids"
- B) "Little Shop of Horrors"
- C) "Flowers for Algernon"
- D) "The Secret Garden"

44. This 1960s culinary innovation was touted as a way to make meals more exciting by cooking everything in gelatin. What was this wobbly phenomenon called?

- A) Aspic Ascendancy
- B) Jello Mania
- C) Gelatinous Gastronomy
- D) Molded Meal Madness

45. In the 1960s, which spy-themed TV show made everyone wish their pen could also be a rocket launcher, or at the very least, a pen?

- A) "I Spy"
- B) "The Man from U.N.C.L.E."
- C) "Mission: Impossible"
- D) "Get Smart"

46. What 1960s fashion trend was both a fire hazard and a statement piece, known for its ability to catch the light and anything else flammable?

- A) Polyester Suits
- B) Lava Lamps as Necklaces
- C) Paper Dresses
- D) Wooden Bead Curtains

47. Which of these was a real beauty trend in the 1960s, ensuring your eyelashes could sweep the floor if you blinked too hard?

- A) Twiggy Lashes
- B) Beehive Hairdos
- C) Go-Go Boots
- D) Mood Rings

48. This 1960s children's toy, based on a simple scientific principle, promised endless hours of fun or at least a solid five minutes until boredom set in. What was it?

- A) The Pet Rock
- B) Silly Putty
- C) The Magic 8-Ball
- D) The Yo-Yo

49. Which 1960s development in automotive technology was thought to be the future of personal transportation, yet somehow didn't catch on as expected?

- A) Electric Cars
- B) The Amphicar (car/boat)
- C) The Monowheel
- D) Flying Cars

50. In the 1960s, this public health campaign aimed to educate about the dangers of smoking with a mascot that was, ironically, a creature known for its heavy breathing. What was it?

- A) Smokey the Bear
- B) Joe Camel
- C) The Marlboro Man
- D) Freddy the Fresh Air Frog

51. Which of these was an actual proposed (but never realized) 1960s project, aiming to provide Americans with a new form of high-speed transportation?

- A) The Underwater Train
- B) The Cross-Country Escalator
- C) The Vacuum Tube Transport System
- D) Hovercraft Commuter Lines

52. Which 1960s innovation was expected to revolutionize personal transportation, yet most people found too exhausting to use for more than a few minutes?

- A) The Pogo Stick
- B) The Skateboard
- C) The Pedal Car
- D) The Unicycle

53. What 1960s "futuristic" household gadget ended up being more of a novelty than a necessity, often relegated to the back of the cupboard?

- A) The Electric Can Opener
- B) The Toaster Oven
- C) The Automatic Egg Cooker
- D) The Soda Siphon

54. Which of these was a real 1960s trend among teenagers, proving that you could indeed wear your emotions on your sleeve, or rather, your finger?

- A) Mood Rings
- B) Friendship Bracelets
- C) Peace Sign Necklaces
- D) Leather Wristbands

55. In the '60s, this was the must-have office gadget for secretaries and writers, touted as the iPad of its day for its portability and style.

- A) The Electric Typewriter
- B) The Stenograph Machine
- C) The Dictaphone
- D) The Slide Rule

56. Which of these 1960s events is often cited as the birth of the modern environmental movement, celebrated annually to encourage acts of green kindness?

- A) Woodstock
- B) The Summer of Love
- C) Earth Day
- D) The Human Be-In

57. This 1960s exercise equipment promised a full-body workout from the comfort of your living room but often ended up as an expensive clothes hanger.

- A) The Stationary Bicycle
- B) The Rowing Machine
- C) The Treadmill
- D) The Exercise Wheel

58. Which of these was a genuine piece of technology developed in the 1960s, aimed at providing homeowners with a new level of security?

- A) The Laser Security System
- B) The Moat and Drawbridge
- C) The Video Doorbell
- D) The Barking Dog Alarm

59. This 1960s toy claimed to predict the future, offering cryptic responses to yes-or-no questions. What was it?

- A) The Magic 8 Ball
- B) The Fortune Teller Fish
- C) The Crystal Ball
- D) The Ouija Board

60. What 1960s food innovation promised convenience but often resulted in a culinary disaster, particularly when instructions weren't followed to the letter?

- A) The Microwave Oven
- B) Instant Mashed Potatoes
- C) The Pop-Up Toaster
- D) Aluminum Foil TV Dinners

HILARIOUS FACTS OF THE 60s

Astronauts Used Hasselblad Cameras with "Space" Film: During the Apollo moon missions in the late 1960s, astronauts were equipped with specially modified Hasselblad cameras to capture the lunar landscape. What's less known is the film inside these cameras was dubbed "moon film" for its ability to withstand the harsh lunar environment. Here's the kicker: some folks back on Earth were so intrigued by this "space film" that they wondered if it could capture ghosts or UFOs back home, given its ability to photograph the unseen lunar surface. Imagine the disappointment when all they got were overexposed shots of the backyard barbecue!

HILARIOUS FACTS OF THE 60s

The Beatles' Submarine Wasn't So Yellow After All: In 1968, the Beatles released "Yellow Submarine," a song and animated movie that captured the imagination of millions. The hilarity lies in the fact that the Beatles themselves had little to do with the movie beyond contributing four new songs and lending their likenesses. The voice actors impersonated the Fab Four throughout the film since the band was initially uninterested in the project. When it became a hit, suddenly, the actual Beatles wanted to be more involved. They hastily filmed a live-action epilogue to be tacked on at the end, making it seem as though they'd been part of the underwater adventure all along. Talk about boarding the submarine just before it docked!

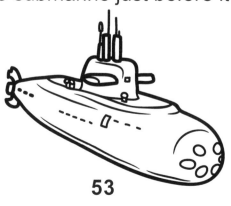

53

HILARIOUS FACTS OF THE 60s

The Great Canadian Coin Snub: In the 1960s, Canada introduced its new, shiny maple leaf flag, a symbol of its distinct identity separate from Britain. Around the same time, the Royal Canadian Mint released a new coin series to celebrate. However, there was one small oversight: the design featured on the coins still included the British Queen with a laurel wreath, reminiscent of Roman emperors, rather than the traditional crown. When Queen Elizabeth II saw the design, she was less than impressed, noting that it made her look like "a cabbage." The mint hurriedly redesigned the coins, but not before "cabbage head" coins made it into circulation, giving Canadians and collectors a leafy piece of numismatic history.

54

HILARIOUS FACTS OF THE 60s

The Spy Who Loved Disguises: The 1960s was the golden age of Cold War espionage, filled with gadgets, disguises, and covert operations. One of the most bizarre spy gadgets from this era was a "turd transmitter." Yes, you read that right. The CIA developed a surveillance device encased in fake dog poop, aptly named "Acoustic Kitty." Agents would place it in strategic locations to eavesdrop on Soviet conversations, banking on the hope that no one would bother picking up what appeared to be dog feces. While the idea was innovative, the practicality was less than stellar, leading to some rather comical situations of agents "planting" their devices in plain sight.

Disco Balls, Bell Bottoms, and the Dawn of the Digital Age: A Groovy Ride Through the 1970s

Welcome to the 1970s—a decade where the pants were wide, the disco balls were shiny, and the hair... oh, the hair was an entity all its own! This was a time when you could stride into a room in platform shoes, under a halo of hairspray, and be the epitome of cool. The '70s were like that one party guest who insists on turning every gathering into a disco dance-off: slightly unpredictable, always entertaining, and with a penchant for dramatic fashion choices.

Picture this: cars were boats on wheels, music was a vinyl-spinning, bass-thumping escapade, and every living room had a shade of orange that hadn't been seen in the wild since.

The era gave us Star Wars, Watergate, and the first personal computer, proving that whether you were aiming to save the galaxy, expose political scandals, or just play Pong in peace, there was something for everyone. Welcome to the 1970s—let's boogie!

1. What was the must-have hairstyle for men in the 1970s?

2. A) The Mohawk

3. B) The Mullet

4. C) The Afro

5. D) The Buzz Cut

2. In 1971, what product did Coca-Cola introduce that flopped because of its name?

- A) New Coke
- B) Coca-Cola Life
- C) Tab Clear
- D) Coca-Cola BlāK

3. Which of the following TV shows did not debut in the 1970s?

- A) MAS*H
- B) The Brady Bunch
- C) Seinfeld
- D) Happy Days

4. In 1974, what peculiar item did over 100 people claim to see flying over New Jersey?

- A) A Giant Potato
- B) A UFO
- C) Santa Claus
- D) The Goodyear Blimp

5. What was the first video game to cause a major craze in arcades and bars during the 1970s?

- A) Space Invaders
- B) Pong
- C) Pac-Man
- D) Asteroids

6. Who famously broke into the Watergate complex, leading to a massive political scandal?

- A) A group of circus performers
- B) Nixon's Plumbers
- C) The FBI
- D) A pack of intelligent raccoons

7. What was the best-selling car in the United States in 1970?
- A) Volkswagen Beetle
- B) Ford Mustang
- C) Chevrolet Impala
- D) AMC Gremlin

8. Which of the following was a popular diet trend in the 1970s?

- A) The Keto Diet
- B) The Atkins Diet
- C) The Grapefruit Diet
- D) Intermittent Fasting

9. Which iconic disco song was actually about a psychiatric hospital?
- A) "Stayin' Alive" by the Bee Gees
- B) "Dancing Queen" by ABBA
- C) "Le Freak" by Chic
- D) "Disco Inferno" by The Trammps

10. What did the first mobile phone in the 1970s weigh?

- A) 2.5 pounds
- B) 4 pounds
- C) 1 pound
- D) 10 pounds

11. What was the name of the first test tube baby, born in 1978?

- A) Elizabeth Holmes
- B) Louise Brown
- C) Mary Shelley
- D) Jane Goodall

12. In 1973, which band released an album that was rumored to be playable at any speed?

- A) The Beatles
- B) Pink Floyd
- C) The Rolling Stones
- D) Monty Python

13. Who famously said, "I did not have sexual relations with that woman," sparking a political uproar in the '70s?
- A) This was actually said in the '90s by Bill Clinton, trick question!
- B) Richard Nixon
- C) Jimmy Carter
- D) Gerald Ford

14. In 1975, an engineer created a digital camera prototype weighing 8 pounds. What was it unable to do?
- A) Take color photos
- B) Save photos digitally
- C) Connect to a computer
- D) Work without a tape recorder

15. Which TV show from the 1970s featured a time-traveling alien?
- A) Battlestar Galactica
- B) Doctor Who
- C) Star Trek
- D) Quantum Leap

16. What did the world fear would run out by the 1980s, according to a 1970s prediction?
- A) Bell-bottom pants
- B) Petroleum
- C) Disco music
- D) Typewriters

17. Which product was invented in the 1970s but became a household necessity in the following decades?
- A) The Microwave Oven
- B) The VCR
- C) Post-it Notes
- D) The Electric Can Opener

18. In the late '70s, what bizarre method was proposed (and seriously considered) to melt the polar ice caps?
- A) Covering them with black soot
- B) Blowing them up with nuclear bombs
- C) Giant space mirrors
- D) None; this is a myth

19. In the 1970s, what did the U.S. government ban for its environmental impact, leading to widespread public outcry?

- A) Aerosol sprays
- B) Lead-based paint
- C) Styrofoam containers
- D) Gasoline-powered cars

20. Which 1970s invention was initially called the "Electronic Babysitter"?

- A) The Television
- B) The Personal Computer
- C) The Video Cassette Recorder (VCR)
- D) The Atari Video Game System

21. What did a group of scientists attempt to teach sign language to in the 1970s?

- A) Dolphins
- B) Gorillas
- C) Chimpanzees
- D) Elephants

22. What unique feature did the 1970s Kodak Instamatic camera introduce to the masses?
- A) Waterproof casing
- B) The selfie stick
- C) Flash cubes
- D) Digital screens

23. Which TV show, debuting in the 1970s, featured a talking car long before "Knight Rider"?
- A) My Mother the Car
- B) The Love Bug
- C) Speed Buggy
- D) Automan

24. Who became the first female prime minister of a country in 1960 and remained a significant political figure through the 1970s?
- A) Indira Gandhi
- B) Golda Meir
- C) Margaret Thatcher
- D) Sirimavo Bandaranaike

25. In the late '70s, which novelty music genre briefly took the world by storm, combining rock and disco?

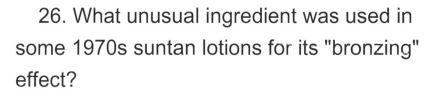

- A) Punk Disco
- B) Disco Rock
- C) Glam Rock
- D) Funk Rock

26. What unusual ingredient was used in some 1970s suntan lotions for its "bronzing" effect?

- A) Coca-Cola
- B) Baby oil
- C) Carrot juice
- D) Coffee grounds

27. In the 1970s, what was the unexpected use of lava lamps beyond home decor?

- A) They were used in scientific experiments.
- B) As a method to encrypt data.
- C) In classrooms to demonstrate volcanic activity.
- D) As mood indicators in office spaces.

28. Which iconic 1970s TV show was originally intended to be a parody of James Bond?
- A) Charlie's Angels
- B) The Six Million Dollar Man
- C) Wonder Woman
- D) Get Smart

29. What was the original purpose of the first mobile phone created in the 1970s?
- A) Military communication
- B) Emergency services
- C) Business transactions
- D) Personal use

30. In 1978, an artist sold an "invisible" art piece. What did the buyer actually receive?
- A) A detailed description of the art
- B) A certificate of ownership
- C) An empty frame
- D) A set of coordinates where the art could be "viewed"

31. What peculiar fitness trend became popular in the 1970s, involving mimicking a farm animal?
- A) Chicken Dance Fitness
- B) Goat Yoga
- C) Prancercise
- D) Duck Waddle Workouts

32. In the 1970s, what did the Viking 1 lander discover when it landed on Mars?
- A) Evidence of water
- B) A "Face on Mars" formation
- C) Martian life forms
- D) A Starbucks

33. Which 1970s song, famous for its unintelligible lyrics, was actually about a dog?
- A) "Louie Louie" by The Kingsmen
- B) "American Pie" by Don McLean
- C) "Blinded by the Light" by Manfred Mann's Earth Band
- D) "Margaritaville" by Jimmy Buffett

34. What was a common yet now unthinkable practice for office workers in the 1970s?
- A) Smoking at their desks
- B) Bringing pets to work
- C) Typing without computers
- D) Working a four-day week

35. What was a popular but dangerous 1970s trend involving children's sleepwear?
- A) Electrically heated pajamas
- B) Glow-in-the-dark pajamas
- C) Flammable nylon pajamas
- D) Pajamas with built-in alarm clocks

36. In the 1970s, a peculiar fashion trend had people wearing what as necklaces?
- A) Mood rings
- B) Live goldfish in tiny bags
- C) Miniature cactus plants
- D) Digital watches

37. What did the creators of the 1970s Pet Rock claim their product was good for?
- A) Guarding the house
- B) Companionship without the mess
- C) Paperweight duties
- D) Educational purposes

38. Which 1970s product was marketed as an "invisible dog leash"?
- A) A stiff wire shaped like a leash
- B) A clear, plastic leash
- C) A retractable leash mechanism
- D) There was no product; it was purely conceptual art

39. During the 1970s, what did the U.S. government experiment with as a form of mail delivery?
- A) Carrier pigeons
- B) Rocket mail
- C) Drone delivery
- D) Subterranean tunnels

40. Which of the following was a real but failed TV pilot from the 1970s?

- A) "Public Morals," a comedy about vice squad cops
- B) "Laser Lawyer," about a lawyer with laser powers
- C) "Supermarket Sweep," a drama set in a grocery store
- D) "The Astronauts' Wives Club," a reality show

41. What bizarre flavor of soda was briefly available in the 1970s?

- A) Celery
- B) Chocolate
- C) Smoked salmon
- D) Garlic

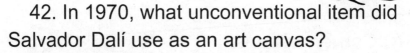

42. In 1970, what unconventional item did Salvador Dalí use as an art canvas?

- A) A tortilla
- B) An entire room
- C) His own body
- D) A television screen

43. What 1970s fitness craze involved sitting and doing nothing?
- A) The "Sit and Be Fit" program
- B) The "Do Nothing" meditation craze
- C) The "Sedentary Lifestyle" movement
- D) "Static Posturing" sessions

44. Which 1970s innovation was mistakenly created while attempting to develop a cure for indigestion?
- A) Bubble wrap
- B) Silly Putty
- C) Non-stick pans
- D) The microwave oven

45. What 1970s band name was inspired by a term for unemployed pilots after World War I?
- A) Led Zeppelin
- B) The Rolling Stones
- C) Fleetwood Mac
- D) Steely Dan

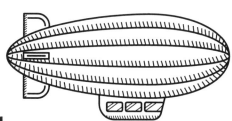

46. Which of the following items was a real product marketed towards fans of the 1970s disco scene?

- A) Disco ball earrings
- B) Glow-in-the-dark dance floor tiles for home use
- C) Portable disco light pens
- D) Edible glitter pills for sparkly bodily functions

47. In the 1970s, a specific type of photography became popular among rock stars, featuring them with what unusual companion?

- A) Their own wax figures
- B) Exotic pets
- C) Haunted house props
- D) Inanimate objects as best friends

48. Which 1970s hit song was actually about the Vietnam War, despite its upbeat tempo?

- A) "Dancing Queen" by ABBA
- B) "Born to Run" by Bruce Springsteen
- C) "Hotel California" by the Eagles
- D) "Fortunate Son" by Creedence Clearwater Revival

49. In 1970s slang, if someone was "laying down a groove," what were they doing?

- A) Sleeping
- B) Dancing
- C) Playing music
- D) Making a phone call

50. What controversial 1970s musical instrument led to a major backlash from traditional musicians?

- A) The synthesizer
- B) The electric guitar
- C) The keytar
- D) The theremin

51. Which of these 1970s "bands" was actually a group of fictional characters from a TV show?

- A) The Partridge Family
- B) The Monkees
- C) Kiss
- D) Pink Floyd

52. The 1970s saw the debut of what would become a legendary rock concert T-shirt, featuring which band?

- A) Led Zeppelin
- B) The Rolling Stones
- C) Pink Floyd
- D) Queen

53. Which iconic 1970s song was written in less than 10 minutes, according to its composer?

- A) "Imagine" by John Lennon
- B) "Bohemian Rhapsody" by Queen
- C) "American Pie" by Don McLean
- D) "Stayin' Alive" by the Bee Gees

54. In the 1970s, which NFL team was known as "The Steel Curtain" for their formidable defense?

- A) Dallas Cowboys
- B) Pittsburgh Steelers
- C) Green Bay Packers
- D) Miami Dolphins

55. Which 1970s NBA player was known for his flamboyant style and once showed up to a game in a Rolls-Royce?
- A) Julius Erving
- B) Wilt Chamberlain
- C) Kareem Abdul-Jabbar
- D) Walt Frazier

56. What unusual event occurred during the 1976 Olympic Games that had never happened before in Olympic history?
- A) A perfect score in gymnastics
- B) The torch went out during the relay
- C) An athlete competed in both the Summer and Winter Olympics in the same year
- D) A summer snowstorm during the opening ceremony

57. Who set the record for the most home runs in a single season in the 1970s, a record that stood for decades?
- A) Hank Aaron
- B) Babe Ruth
- C) Roger Maris
- D) Barry Bonds   75

58. What groundbreaking technology was introduced during the 1976 Winter Olympics, changing the way viewers experienced sports broadcasts?

- A) Instant replay
- B) Underwater cameras
- C) 3D television broadcasting
- D) Color TV broadcasting

59. In the 1970s, which world leader famously claimed to have beaten 50,000 people in chess simultaneously?

- A) Fidel Castro
- B) Leonid Brezhnev
- C) Muammar Gaddafi
- D) Henry Kissinger

60. During the 1970s, a new dance craze swept across discos worldwide, known for its line of participants mimicking a train. What was it called?

- A) The Funky Chicken
- B) The Disco Train
- C) The Hustle
- D) The Electric Slide

HILARIOUS FACTS OF THE 70s

The Great Disco Demolition Night: In 1979, at the height of the disco era, an event called "Disco Demolition Night" took place at Comiskey Park in Chicago. The idea was simple: fans were encouraged to bring disco records to a doubleheader baseball game, between games the records would be blown up in a crate at center field. The event, meant to purge the world of disco music, turned chaotic. Thousands of fans stormed the field after the explosion, causing such a mess that the Chicago White Sox had to forfeit the second game due to the damage. This event marked the symbolic "death" of disco and remains one of the most bizarre promotional stunts gone wrong in sports history.

HILARIOUS FACTS OF THE 70s

Rock 'n' Roll Meets the White House:
When Elvis Presley visited President Richard Nixon at the White House in December 1970, the meeting between the King of Rock 'n' Roll and the leader of the free world was as surreal as it gets. Elvis showed up unannounced, seeking to be appointed a "Federal Agent-at-Large" in the Bureau of Narcotics and Dangerous Drugs because he was concerned about the drug culture affecting the youth. Nixon, somewhat perplexed by the request, still took the meeting. The iconic photo of their handshake is a testament to one of the most unusual friendships of the 1970s. Elvis left with a federal narcotics badge, and Nixon got a bit more street cred with the younger generation. Talk about an odd couple!.

HILARIOUS FACTS OF THE 70s

The Accidental President's Dog Speechwriter: In the 1970s, the presidential pet was often as much a celebrity as the president himself. President Gerald Ford's golden retriever, Liberty, was no exception and unwittingly became part of a humorous incident. During a press conference, Ford jokingly remarked that his speeches were actually written by Liberty. The media ran with the story, and for a brief moment, the nation was captivated by the idea of a dog contributing to national policy discussions. The image of Liberty pawing over speech drafts added a light-hearted moment to Ford's presidency.

79

HILARIOUS FACTS OF THE 70s

The Accidental Invention of the Ultimate Snack: In the 1970s, a chef at the Toll House Inn in Whitman, Massachusetts, ran out of baker's chocolate while making cookies. In a pinch, she chopped up a bar of Nestle semi-sweet chocolate, expecting it to melt and disperse through the cookie dough. Instead, the chocolate pieces held their shape, and the chocolate chip cookie was born. Nestle was so impressed that they struck a deal with her: her cookie recipe would be printed on the packaging of their chocolate bars in exchange for a lifetime supply of chocolate. Little did they know, they had just created what would become America's favorite cookie, all because of a culinary improvisation.

Neon Lights, Knight Riders, and Cassette Plights: A Totally Tubular Trip Through the 1980s

Ah, the 1980s—a decade so bright, you needed shades just to open the fridge. It was a time when hair volume was directly proportional to one's social status, and leg warmers weren't just for legs anymore (they were for fashion, darling). The '80s gave us the magic of the mullet, where business in the front and party in the back wasn't just a hairstyle; it was a way of life.

Picture this: You're walking down the street, a Walkman strapped to your hip, blasting synth-pop so powerful it could resurrect a Tamagotchi. On the corner, there's a group of kids trading Garbage Pail Kids cards like they're stocks on Wall Street. And just down the block, a neon arcade palace beckons with the seductive bleeps and bloops of Pac-Man and Space Invaders.

The '80s were when movies were radical, music videos were king, and everyone was just a Thriller night away from turning into a zombie or a backup dancer for Michael Jackson. It was a decade where you could save the universe in your underwear (thanks to video games, not actual cosmic responsibilities) and where the most heated debates weren't about politics... they were about whether VHS or Betamax would win the video war.

So tease up that hair, grab your brightest neon spandex, and let's moonwalk through the decade that brought us the Rubik's Cube, E.T., and the unforgettable battle cry: "I want my MTV!" Welcome to the 1980s!

1. Which product, introduced in the 1980s, was initially feared to harm record sales?

- A) The Walkman
- B) The VCR
- C) The CD Player
- D) The Cassette Tape

2. In the 1980s, what did the term "yuppie" refer to?

- A) A type of fast-food burger
- B) Young urban professionals
- C) A new genre of music
- D) A children's toy

3. What was the best-selling video game of the 1980s?

- A) Super Mario Bros.
- B) Tetris
- C) Pac-Man
- D) The Legend of Zelda

4. Which 1980s movie popularized the phrase "I'll be back"?
- A) Back to the Future
- B) The Terminator
- C) Ghostbusters
- D) Die Hard

5. What unusual fitness trend became wildly popular in the 1980s?
- A) Jazzercise
- B) Hula hooping
- C) Prancercising
- D) Aerobics with farm animals

6. Which 1980s TV show featured a car that could talk and drive itself?
- A) Magnum P.I.
- B) Knight Rider
- C) The A-Team
- D) Miami Vice

7. In 1985, Coca-Cola made a controversial change to its formula, calling it:
- A) Diet Coke
- B) Coke II
- C) New Coke
- D) Crystal Pepsi

8. Which 1980s fashion trend involved wearing socks over leggings?
- A) Punk
- B) Goth
- C) Preppy
- D) Aerobic Chic

9. Who was the first woman appointed to the United States Supreme Court in the 1980s?
- A) Ruth Bader Ginsburg
- B) Sandra Day O'Connor
- C) Sonia Sotomayor
- D) Elena Kagan

10. What was the original purpose of the Internet, which began to be developed in the 1980s?
- A) Social Media
- B) Military Communications
- C) Online Shopping
- D) Streaming Music

11. In the 1980s, this board game, which involves solving a murder mystery, was turned into a feature film:
- A) Monopoly
- B) Scrabble
- C) Clue (Cluedo)
- D) Risk

12. Which iconic 1980s song was originally written as a slow ballad before becoming a pop hit?
- A) "Girls Just Want to Have Fun" by Cyndi Lauper
- B) "Billie Jean" by Michael Jackson
- C) "Like a Virgin" by Madonna
- D) "Every Breath You Take" by The Police

13. What was the name of the first Space Shuttle launched by NASA in the 1980s?
- A) Challenger
- B) Discovery
- C) Atlantis
- D) Columbia

14. Which 1980s invention was crucial for the development of the personal computer?
- A) The microprocessor
- B) The floppy disk
- C) The mouse
- D) The graphical user interface (GUI)

15. In 1980, who became the youngest male winner of a Grand Slam singles title in tennis?
- A) John McEnroe
- B) Bjorn Borg
- C) Andre Agassi
- D) Boris Becker

16. What did the "Brat Pack" refer to in the 1980s?
- A) A group of popular high school students
- B) A brand of children's lunch snacks
- C) A collective of young, up-and-coming actors
- D) A new wave band

17. Which 1980s TV series was famous for its narrated introductions by an unseen billionaire, recruiting people to solve crimes?
- A) Dallas
- B) Dynasty
- C) Magnum, P.I.
- D) Charlie's Angels

18. The Rubik's Cube, a puzzle invented in the 1970s, became an iconic toy of the 1980s. What was its original purpose?
- A) A teaching tool for mathematics
- B) A test of intelligence for job interviews
- C) A prototype for a new type of storage cube
- D) A paperweight

19. Which 1980s movie was the first to use CGI (Computer Generated Imagery) for its special effects?
- A) Tron
- B) Blade Runner
- C) The Last Starfighter
- D) Star Wars: The Empire Strikes Back

20. In the late 1980s, a global environmental campaign focused on saving what specific area?
- A) The Amazon Rainforest
- B) The Great Barrier Reef
- C) The Sahara Desert
- D) The Arctic Circle

21. What groundbreaking product did Apple Inc. introduce in 1984?
- A) The iPod
- B) The MacBook
- C) The iPhone
- D) The Macintosh

22. Which of the following video games did not debut in the 1980s?
- A) Tetris
- B) Super Mario Bros.
- C) Pac-Man
- D) Halo

23. The 1980s saw the first woman to be inducted into the Rock and Roll Hall of Fame. Who was she?
- A) Aretha Franklin
- B) Madonna
- C) Janis Joplin
- D) Tina Turner

24. In 1983, President Ronald Reagan proposed a missile defense system that was popularly dubbed as:
- A) Star Wars
- B) Sky Shield
- C) Moonraker
- D) Star Trek

25. Which 1980s film was the first to have its theme park ride?
- A) Back to the Future
- B) E.T. the Extra-Terrestrial
- C) Ghostbusters
- D) Indiana Jones

26. Who broke the world record for the fastest marathon in the 1980s, setting a new standard in long-distance running?
- A) Steve Jones
- B) Carlos Lopes
- C) Alberto Salazar
- D) Rob de Castella

27. In the 1980s, which company was the first to develop and sell a cell phone?
- A) Nokia
- B) Motorola
- C) Sony
- D) Samsung

28. The 1980s fashion trend of "power dressing" was symbolized by:
- A) Neon colors and leg warmers
- B) Leather jackets and ripped jeans
- C) Suits with broad shoulder pads
- D) Tie-dye shirts and bell-bottoms

29. Who became the first woman in space in 1983?
- A) Valentina Tereshkova
- B) Sally Ride
- C) Mae Jemison
- D) Judith Resnik

30. The 1980s saw the rise of "designer jeans." Which of the following brands was not a key player in this trend?
- A) Calvin Klein
- B) Levi Strauss
- C) Gucci
- D) Gloria Vanderbilt

31. In the realm of 1980s pop culture, what was Max Headroom?
- A) A hit single by a New Wave band
- B) A computer-generated TV host
- C) A famous skateboard trick
- D) A fictional soda brand

32. Which iconic 1980s movie featured a soundtrack that became almost as famous as the film itself, featuring the hit "Don't You (Forget About Me)"?
- A) Ferris Bueller's Day Off
- B) The Breakfast Club
- C) Top Gun
- D) Flashdance

33. Which 1980s fashion trend involved people wearing oversized tops that hung off one shoulder?
- A) The grunge look
- B) Power dressing
- C) The preppy look
- D) The Flashdance effect

34. Which iconic 1980s product was famously advertised with the slogan "Is it live, or is it Memorex?"
- A) VHS Tapes
- B) Cassette Tapes
- C) CD Players
- D) Record Players

35. Who became the first female Prime Minister of the United Kingdom in 1979 and served throughout the 1980s?
- A) Margaret Thatcher
- B) Elizabeth II
- C) Indira Gandhi
- D) Angela Merkel

36. The 1980s saw the rise of what musical genre, characterized by synthesizers and a futuristic sound?
- A) Punk Rock
- B) Heavy Metal
- C) New Wave
- D) Reggae

37. Which 1980s film popularized the concept of a "teen movie" and was directed by John Hughes?

- A) Ferris Bueller's Day Off
- B) The Breakfast Club
- C) Sixteen Candles
- D) All of the above

38. What was the name of the international agreement signed in 1987 to protect the ozone layer by phasing out the production of numerous substances believed to be responsible for ozone depletion?

- A) The Paris Agreement
- B) The Kyoto Protocol
- C) The Montreal Protocol
- D) The Stockholm Convention

39. What did Ronald Reagan famously joke about during a microphone check, causing a brief moment of panic in 1984?

- A) "I've decided to switch parties."
- B) "We begin bombing in five minutes."
- C) "I forgot where I left the nuclear codes."
- D) "I've signed legislation outlawing the Soviet Union."

40. Which fashion item became a surprising DIY trend in the 1980s after people started ripping their clothes on purpose?

- A) Turtlenecks
- B) Jeans
- C) Sweatshirts
- D) Socks

41. Which of these was a real but ill-fated fashion trend of the 1980s?

- A) Inflatable hats
- B) Shoulder pad inserts for t-shirts
- C) Neon leg warmers for pets
- D) Parachute pants

42. The 1980s introduced the world to the "talking" car in "Knight Rider." What was the car's name?

- A) KITT
- B) KARR
- C) AUTO
- D) VOICE

43. In the 1980s, which fitness guru encouraged us to "feel the burn" long before it became a political catchphrase?

- A) Arnold Schwarzenegger
- B) Richard Simmons
- C) Jane Fonda
- D) Lou Ferrigno

44. In the 1980s, what did teenagers often do on Friday nights, now a nearly exlinct social activity?

- A) Disco dancing
- B) Watching live TV broadcasts
- C) Going to the video rental store
- D) Sending telegrams to each other

45. In the 1980s, what did many people start wearing on their wrists, not to tell time, but as a fashion statement?

- A) Swatch Watches
- B) Rolex Watches
- C) Rubber Bands
- D) Live Strong Bracelets

46. In the 1980s, this beverage claimed to be "The Choice of a New Generation."
- A) Coca-Cola
- B) Pepsi
- C) Tab
- D) New York Seltzer

47. Which 1980s movie made dancing in an abandoned warehouse seem like the ultimate form of rebellion?

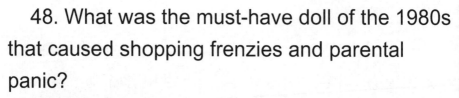

- A) Dirty Dancing
- B) Flashdance
- C) Footloose
- D) Fame

48. What was the must-have doll of the 1980s that caused shopping frenzies and parental panic?
- A) Barbie
- B) Cabbage Patch Kids
- C) My Little Pony
- D) G.I. Joe

49. In the 1980s, what video game did parents accuse of causing "arcade fever" and depleting allowances everywhere?

- A) Donkey Kong
- B) Space Invaders
- C) Pac-Man
- D) Tetris

50. The 1980s introduced us to the concept of music television. What was the first music video aired on MTV?

- A) Michael Jackson - "Thriller"
- B) Madonna - "Like a Virgin"
- C) The Buggles - "Video Killed the Radio Star"
- D) A-ha - "Take On Me"

51. In the world of 1980s television, which show featured a wealthy oil tycoon family that defined prime-time soap drama?

- A) The Waltons
- B) Dynasty
- C) Dallas
- D) Falcon Crest

99

52. Which of these was a popular 1980s snack that promised a "fruit snack" experience but was mostly sugar?
- A) Fruit Roll-Ups
- B) Carrot Sticks
- C) Dried Apricots
- D) Celery with Peanut Butter

53. What was the epitome of cool transportation for kids in the 1980s, second only to the DeLorean?
- A) The BMX Bike
- B) Rollerblades
- C) Skateboard
- D) Pogo Stick

54. In the 1980s, what was every kid's dream machine, capable of making sweet, frozen treats at home?
- A) The Ice Cream Maker
- B) The Snow Cone Machine
- C) The Popsicle Mold
- D) The Frozen Yogurt Dispenser

55. What was the iconic fashion statement involving footwear in the 1980s, especially among teens?

- A) Wearing two different colored socks
- B) High-heeled sneakers
- C) Sandals with socks
- D) Glowing sneakers

56. Which 1980s cultural phenomenon involved people trying to solve a crime by dining and watching a play simultaneously?

- A) Dinner Theater
- B) Murder Mystery Parties
- C) Drive-In Movie Theaters
- D) Reality TV Shows

57. Which iconic 1980s TV show featured an extraterrestrial who loved to eat cats?

- A) Mork & Mindy
- B) ALF
- C) Star Trek: The Next Generation
- D) Quantum Leap

58. In the 1980s, this fashion accessory became an unexpected symbol of punk rock rebellion. What was it?
- A) Safety pins
- B) Neon headbands
- C) Oversized earrings
- D) Leather bracelets

59. Which 1980s event became a defining moment for live music broadcasts, featuring a reunited Led Zeppelin?
- A) Woodstock '89
- B) The first Lollapalooza
- C) Live Aid
- D) The US Festival

60. What was the ultimate status symbol for teens and young adults in the 1980s, often used to create the perfect mixtape?
- A) The Boombox
- B) The Walkman
- C) The Discman
- D) The Record Player

HILARIOUS FACTS OF THE 80s

The Cola Wars' Space Front: In the mid-1980s, the "Cola Wars" between Coca-Cola and Pepsi reached new heights—literally. Both companies were so eager to prove their soda's superiority that they took their rivalry into space. In 1985, Pepsi and Coca-Cola each developed special cans to be used by astronauts in zero gravity aboard the Space Shuttle Challenger. The idea was to allow astronauts to enjoy their favorite sodas while orbiting Earth. The endeavor wasn't just a small step for man, but a giant leap for soda-kind. However, the astronauts were less than impressed; the lack of gravity affected the sodas' taste and carbonation, leading to a rather flat experience. This space soda mission may not have won the cola wars, but it certainly earned a place in the annals of quirky marketing stunts.

103

HILARIOUS FACTS OF THE 80s

When Video Games Met Aerobics: The 1980s were not only the golden age of arcade video games but also the era of aerobics, complete with leg warmers and headbands. In a fusion of these two cultural phenomena, the world saw the release of the "Dance Aerobics" game for the Nintendo Entertainment System in 1987. Players used a floor mat controller to step and jump in time with on-screen instructions, effectively turning their living room into an aerobics studio. The game intended to make exercise fun by combining it with the video game craze. However, the sight of gamers jumping around to electronic beeps while trying not to trip over the NES cords was more comedic than athletic. "Dance Aerobics" remains a whimsical footnote in the history of fitness and gaming, highlighting the decade's penchant for blending technology with exercise in the most amusing ways.

HILARIOUS FACTS OF THE 80s

The Great Garbage Barge Odyssey: In 1987, a barge named the Mobro 4000 became unexpectedly famous, carrying 3,168 tons of New York's garbage. The barge set sail to find a place to dump its load but was turned away by every port, from North Carolina to Belize. For five months, the barge wandered the seas, rejected everywhere it went, becoming an unlikely media sensation and a floating symbol of the era's environmental challenges. The saga highlighted the growing problem of waste disposal and sparked conversations about recycling and waste management. It's a tale that perhaps unintentionally taught us all a lesson about the importance of taking out the trash— just not on a global sea tour.

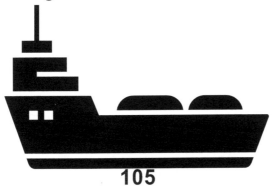

HILARIOUS FACTS OF THE 80s

When Pets Predicted the Weather: In the 1980s, before the internet and smartphone apps made weather forecasts available at our fingertips, some TV stations employed unconventional methods to predict the weather. One station in the US famously used a groundhog, but in the UK, a station briefly experimented with a "weather predicting" leech named Gronwyn. According to folklore, the behavior of leeches in a jar could forecast the weather, and Gronwyn was put on TV to make predictions. While Gronwyn's accuracy was questionable at best, the leech did enjoy a brief moment of fame as perhaps the only weather forecaster to work for food—blood, that is. This quirky episode serves as a reminder of how far we've come in meteorological science and television programming.

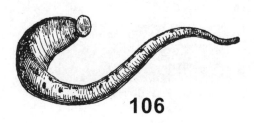

Dial-Up Dreams and Flannel Schemes: A Zany Zip Through the 1990s

Ah, the 1990s—a decade where the internet went "eeee-errrr-ahhhhh" and fashion was a wild mix of neon, flannel, and not nearly enough regret. This was the era where cartoons were king and breakfast cereals were more sugar than cereal. If you weren't trying to solve the mystery of the Magic Eye posters (it's a sailboat, by the way), you were probably feeding your Tamagotchi or mourning its untimely death because, let's face it, those things were high maintenance.

Remember when being "online" meant nobody could call your house? Those were the days when "You've got mail!" was an exciting novelty, not an overflowing digital chore. The '90s gave us the gift of grunge music, where the lyrics were as incomprehensible as our teenage moods, and the biggest dilemma was whether to put your trust in VHS or bet everything on LaserDisc.

107

This was a time when cell phones were the size of a brick—if you were lucky enough to have one—and the concept of privacy was leaving the family computer in the living room, hoping nobody would stumble upon your AOL chat rooms.

In the '90s, when every kid knew the Macarena but didn't understand why, and the ultimate status symbol was having the freshest pair of light-up sneakers.

So, let's rewind the tape, adjust the rabbit ears on the TV, and take a nostalgic trip back to the '90s. And remember, be kind, rewind!

1. Which '90s toy became a global craze, often blamed for classroom distractions due to its constant need for care?
- A) Beanie Babies
- B) Furby
- C) Tamagotchi
- D) Pogs

2. In the '90s, what was the must-have accessory for every "cool" tech user, often resulting in tangled wires and lost earbuds?
- A) The Discman
- B) The Walkman
- C) Pager
- D) The first iPod

3. What infamous '90s fashion trend essentially involved wearing underwear as outerwear?
- A) Crop tops
- B) Flannel shirts
- C) Baggy jeans
- D) Slip dresses

109

4. Which '90s TV show popularized the phrase "How you doin'?"?
- A) Seinfeld
- B) Friends
- C) Frasier
- D) The Fresh Prince of Bel-Air

5. Which '90s food fad was essentially just a clear version of its original and baffled consumers with its purpose?
- A) Crystal Pepsi
- B) Fat-free chips
- C) Green ketchup
- D) Purple mustard

6. In the 1990s, this video game character became an icon, known for his speed and collecting rings:
- A) Mario
- B) Sonic the Hedgehog
- C) Link
- D) Mega Man

7. What was the first movie to be released on DVD in the United States, marking the beginning of the end for VHS tapes?

- A) The Matrix
- B) Titanic
- C) Twister
- D) Jurassic Park

8. In the late '90s, which Internet service was infamous for sending out a seemingly endless supply of free trial CDs?

- A) Netscape
- B) AOL
- C) MSN
- D) Yahoo!

9. Which '90s phenomenon involved dancing in a line, making it a staple at weddings and school dances alike?

- A) The Macarena
- B) The Electric Slide
- C) The Cha Cha Slide
- D) The Tootsee Roll

10. In the 1990s, which snack was famously advertised by a cartoon tiger, urging kids to consider them "G-r-r-reat!"?
- A) Cheetos
- B) Frosted Flakes
- C) Fruit Gushers
- D) Pop-Tarts

11. Which iconic 1990s device promised personal organization but ended up being most people's glorified address book?
- A) The Palm Pilot
- B) The Nokia 3310
- C) The Game Boy Color
- D) The Tamagotchi

12. In the realm of '90s fashion, what was the fate of most flannel shirts?
- A) Worn strictly for warmth
- B) Used as a makeshift belt
- C) Tied around the waist
- D) Converted into headwear

13. What was the "must-have" Beanie Baby that drove collectors into a frenzy in the 1990s?
- A) Patti the Platypus
- B) Princess the Bear
- C) Legs the Frog
- D) Peace the Bear

14. Which '90s music group was known for their matching outfits and choreographed dance moves?

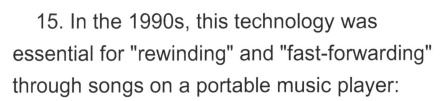

- A) Nirvana
- B) Spice Girls
- C) Backstreet Boys
- D) Metallica

15. In the 1990s, this technology was essential for "rewinding" and "fast-forwarding" through songs on a portable music player:
- A) Bluetooth connectivity
- B) Touch screen
- C) Cassette tape
- D) Voice control

16. What was the name of the '90s TV show that made an educational adventure out of chasing a villain through time and space?
- A) Where in the World Is Carmen Sandiego?
- B) Bill Nye the Science Guy
- C) The Magic School Bus
- D) Reading Rainbow

17. Which '90s fashion item was notorious for being uncomfortable but was worn by both men and women in an attempt to look cool?
- A) The bodysuit
- B) Platform shoes
- C) Butterfly clips
- D) Choker necklaces

18. The '90s saw the birth of the Internet meme, with this funny baby becoming an early viral sensation. What was its nickname?
- A) Cha-Cha Baby
- B) Boogie Baby
- C) Baby Groove
- D) Dancing Baby

19. In the '90s, which technology was infamously known for its loud screeching sound while connecting to the Internet?

- A) Dial-up Modem
- B) CD-ROM Drive
- C) Floppy Disk Drive
- D) Dot Matrix Printer

20. Which '90s movie inspired a generation to shout "There's no crying in baseball!"?

- A) Major League
- B) The Sandlot
- C) A League of Their Own
- D) Field of Dreams

21. What was the must-have office software of the '90s, known for its helpful but often annoying assistant, Clippy?

- A) Microsoft Word
- B) Microsoft Excel
- C) Microsoft PowerPoint
- D) Microsoft Office

22. The '90s introduced this controversial toy that parents feared would turn their children into anarchists. What was it?

- A) Furby
- B) Troll dolls
- C) Beanie Babies
- D) Giga Pets

23. Which '90s drink was marketed as a fruit-flavored soda for the "next generation" but ended up being a flop?

- A) Crystal Pepsi
- B) Surge
- C) Josta
- D) Orbitz

24. What '90s phenomenon involved collecting and trading shiny, illustrated pieces of cardboard, leading to playground trades and even thefts?

- A) Garbage Pail Kids
- B) Pokémon Cards
- C) Pogs
- D) Beanie Babies

25. Which '90s movie famously featured a young computer hacker who finds himself inside a digital world?
- A) Tron
- B) Hackers
- C) The Matrix
- D) Johnny Mnemonic

26. The '90s saw the rise of a dance craze based on a song that instructed listeners to slide, crisscross, and cha-cha. What was it?
- A) The Macarena
- B) The Electric Slide
- C) The Cha Cha Slide
- D) The Cupid Shuffle

27. Which of these was a must-have '90s fashion accessory that no self-respecting teen would be caught without?
- A) Feathered boas
- B) Mood rings
- C) Scrunchies
- D) Elbow gloves

28. In the '90s, what was the ultimate symbol of office modernity, capable of sending a document over the phone line?

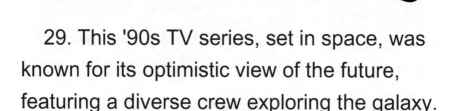

- A) The pager
- B) The fax machine
- C) The photocopier
- D) The desktop computer

29. This '90s TV series, set in space, was known for its optimistic view of the future, featuring a diverse crew exploring the galaxy.

- A) Battlestar Galactica
- B) Babylon 5
- C) Star Trek: The Next Generation
- D) The X-Files

30. In the 1990s, this car became synonymous with reliability and affordability, becoming a staple in high school parking lots.

- A) Ford Mustang
- B) Honda Civic
- C) Chevrolet Camaro
- D) Volkswagen Beetle

31. Which NBA team dominated the 1990s by winning six championships during the decade?

- A) Los Angeles Lakers
- B) Chicago Bulls
- C) Boston Celtics
- D) Detroit Pistons

32. The 1990s music scene was marked by the emergence of grunge. Which city is considered the birthplace of grunge music?

- A) Los Angeles, California
- B) New York City, New York
- C) Seattle, Washington
- D) Austin, Texas

33. In 1999, the Women's World Cup sparked increased interest in women's soccer in the United States. Which player famously removed her shirt in celebration after scoring the winning penalty kick in the final?

- A) Mia Hamm
- B) Brandi Chastain
- C) Julie Foudy
- D) Abby Wambach

34. Which 1990s TV show, known for its cultural impact on fashion and lifestyle, featured a group of friends living in New York City?

- A) Seinfeld
- B) Friends
- C) The Fresh Prince of Bel-Air
- D) Frasier

35. The 1990s saw the rise of electronic dance music (EDM). Which of these acts was pivotal in bringing EDM to mainstream audiences?

- A) The Prodigy
- B) Nirvana
- C) Spice Girls
- D) Backstreet Boys

36. The "Unplugged" series on MTV was a hallmark of '90s music culture. Which artist's "Unplugged" performance became particularly legendary, released posthumously in 1994?

- A) Kurt Cobain (Nirvana)
- B) Eric Clapton
- C) Lauryn Hill
- D) Alice in Chains

37. What major event in the world of chess took place in 1997, highlighting the advancement of artificial intelligence?

- A) Deep Blue, an IBM computer, defeated world champion Garry Kasparov.
- B) The introduction of the first chess-playing robot.
- C) The founding of the Online Chess Federation.
- D) The first use of computer analysis in a world championship match.

38. Which of these fashion items became an unexpected symbol of '90s youth culture, particularly associated with the skateboarding scene?

- A) Baggy cargo pants
- B) Plaid flannel shirts
- C) Bucket hats
- D) Wallet chains

39. Which artist famously changed his name to an unpronounceable symbol in the 1990s?

- A) Prince
- B) Madonna
- C) David Bowie
- D) George Michael

40. The 1990s saw the first publication of a book series that would become a global phenomenon, chronicling the adventures of a young wizard. What series was it?

- A) The Lord of the Rings
- B) Harry Potter
- C) Percy Jackson
- D) The Chronicles of Narnia

41. In 1997, Tiger Woods won his first major championship by setting a record-breaking score. Which tournament did he win?

- A) The Open Championship
- B) The Masters
- C) The U.S. Open
- D) The PGA Championship

42. Which female tennis player dominated the 1990s by winning 22 Grand Slam singles titles during her career?

- A) Martina Navratilova
- B) Monica Seles
- C) Steffi Graf
- D) Serena Williams

43. In the world of movies, the 1990s introduced us to CGI as a mainstay in film production. Which 1993 movie is often credited with revolutionizing the use of CGI in cinema?

- A) Toy Story
- B) Terminator 2: Judgment Day
- C) Jurassic Park
- D) The Matrix

44. The 1990s grunge scene was as much about music as it was about fashion. Which of these items was least likely to be worn by grunge enthusiasts?

- A) Flannel shirts
- B) Doc Martens boots
- C) Baggy jeans
- D) Bright neon leotards

45. The 1990s rap scene was marked by the East Coast-West Coast rivalry. Which of these artists was associated with the East Coast rap scene?

- A) Tupac Shakur
- B) Snoop Dogg
- C) Dr. Dre
- D) The Notorious B.I.G.

46. "Friends" was one of the most popular TV shows of the 1990s. Which coffee shop was the gang's regular hangout spot?

- A) Central Perk
- B) The Peach Pit
- C) Monk's Café
- D) The Max

47. Which iconic 1990s TV series featured a group of high school students and their principal, Mr. Belding?

- A) Beverly Hills, 90210
- B) Dawson's Creek
- C) Saved by the Bell
- D) Boy Meets World

48. In 1996, this product was dubbed the "toy of the year," leading to holiday shopping frenzies across the United States. What was it?

- A) Furby
- B) Tickle Me Elmo
- C) Beanie Babies
- D) Tamagotchi

49. Michael Jordan retired for the first time from professional basketball during the 1990s. Which sport did he briefly switch to?
- A) Baseball
- B) Golf
- C) Football
- D) Boxing

50. The 1990s saw the rise of several iconic female vocalists. Which artist released the album "Jagged Little Pill," one of the decade's best-selling albums?
- A) Alanis Morissette
- B) Mariah Carey
- C) Madonna
- D) Whitney Houston

51. Which '90s movie, centered around a board game, brought wild animals and other jungle elements to life in the real world?
- A) Jumanji
- B) The Lion King
- C) Jurassic Park
- D) Toy Story

52. In 1992, this device became a must-have for music lovers, allowing them to carry their favorite tunes on the go, before the digital revolution.

- A) Sony Walkman
- B) Sony Discman
- C) iPod
- D) MP3 Player

53. This '90s TV show broke new ground by being the first animated primetime series since "The Flintstones" to be nominated for a Primetime Emmy Award for Outstanding Comedy Series.

- A) The Simpsons
- B) South Park
- C) Family Guy
- D) King of the Hill

54. The 1990s tech boom led to the creation of many internet companies, known as "dot-coms." Which of these was not a '90s internet startup?

- A) Amazon
- B) Google
- C) Facebook
- D) eBay

55. In 1998, this breakthrough medication was approved by the FDA, becoming a cultural phenomenon and the subject of countless jokes and commercials.

- A) Prozac
- B) Viagra
- C) Lipitor
- D) Zoloft

56. The '90s were known for their public health campaigns, including this memorable slogan aimed at children to promote drug awareness.

- A) "Just Say No"
- B) "D.A.R.E. to Resist Drugs and Violence"
- C) "Hugs Not Drugs"
- D) "This Is Your Brain on Drugs"

57. One of the biggest sports scandals of the 1990s involved an attack on figure skater Nancy Kerrigan. Who was associated with planning the attack?

- A) Tonya Harding
- B) Michelle Kwan
- C) Kristi Yamaguchi
- D) Oksana Baiul

58. The 1990s saw the introduction of this groundbreaking piece of technology, allowing users to "burn" their own CDs for the first time. What was it?

- A) CD-ROM Drive
- B) CD Writer
- C) Floppy Disk
- D) VHS Recorder

59. This '90s game show featured contestants performing stunts and answering questions to win prizes, famously hosted by Marc Summers.

- A) Double Dare
- B) The Price Is Right
- C) Wheel of Fortune
- D) Jeopardy!

60. Who famously broke the home run record in 1998, a record that had stood for 37 years?

- A) Sammy Sosa
- B) Barry Bonds
- C) Mark McGwire
- D) Ken Griffey Jr.

HILARIOUS FACTS OF THE 90s

The Infamous Tamagotchi Pet Cemeteries: In the late 1990s, the Tamagotchi, a handheld digital pet, became a global craze among kids and even adults. The goal was to nurture your pixelated pet, but failure to properly care for it would lead to its demise. This led to a somewhat bizarre and unexpectedly hilarious phenomenon: the creation of online Tamagotchi cemeteries. Yes, virtual graveyards where grieving owners could commemorate their digital companions with epitaphs. Some took it further, holding actual funerals for their pets, complete with eulogies. It was a time of mourning and reflection... over the loss of a few pixels on a screen.

HILARIOUS FACTS OF THE 90s

The Great Beanie Baby Investment Bubble: The 1990s witnessed the peculiar economic bubble of Beanie Babies. These plush toys, produced by Ty Inc., were originally sold as children's gifts, but adults soon caught on to the craze, convinced that these stuffed animals would become valuable collectors' items in the future. People invested thousands of dollars in Beanie Babies, trading them like stocks, and some even used them as collateral for loans! The bubble burst towards the end of the decade, leaving many with vast collections of cuddly critters that weren't quite the goldmine they'd hoped for. The episode remains one of the most whimsical examples of speculative investment gone awry.

HILARIOUS FACTS OF THE 90s

The Presidential Sax Solo that Rocked the Vote: In 1992, during his campaign for the U.S. presidency, Bill Clinton made an appearance on "The Arsenio Hall Show" that would become one of the most memorable moments of the election. Dressed not in his usual suit and tie but in a cool pair of sunglasses, Clinton played "Heartbreak Hotel" on his saxophone, accompanied by the show's band. This performance not only showcased Clinton's musical chops but also helped to solidify his image as a relatable and charismatic candidate. It's said that his saxophone solo played a part in swaying the younger demographic, proving that sometimes, all you need to win votes is a smooth jazz riff and a pair of shades.

The Left-Handed Whopper Debacle:

On April 1, 1998, Burger King announced the introduction of a new menu item tailored for the 32 million left-handed Americans: the "Left-Handed Whopper." This innovative burger was designed to have all condiments rotated 180 degrees, supposedly to benefit left-handed burger aficionados. The ad assured that the new burger would prevent spillage from the other side for left-handers. The announcement was, of course, an April Fools' joke, but it resulted in thousands of customers flocking to Burger King restaurants to try the new burger. The following day, Burger King issued a reveal, admitting the hoax, but not before right-handed customers had begun requesting their own version. It was a prank that left both customers and employees in stitches, and remains a delicious slice of '90s fast-food folklore.

ANSWERS 1950s

1. B) Sea-Monkeys
2. D) Cootie catcher
3. A) A color TV
4. B) A drive-in movie theater
5. C) The Vibrating Belt Machine
6. A) A weather rock
7. D) The Bouffant
8. C) "My Favorite Martian"
9. D) Poodle Skirts
10. B) Blue Jeans
11. B) The Hi-Fi Record Player
12. D) The Jetpack
13. A) The Grapefruit Diet
14. C) Cruising
15. C) The Freeze
16. B) The Electric Can Opener
17. B) Freeze-Dried Ice Cream
18. B) The 20-Foot Phone Cord
19. C) T-shirts and Jeans
20. A) Sleep Learning Records
21. A) Smell-O-Vision
22. D) Ham and Pineapple Skewers
23. C) The Dishwasher

24. B) Cat-Eye Glasses

25. A) The Charcoal Grill

26. B) Lucy Ricardo

27. C) Televisionitis

28. C) Air Conditioning

29. A) Captain Video

30. D) Pink Shirts

31. C) Lady and the Tramp

32. B) Play-Doh

33. A) Godzilla

34. D) SPAM Pizza

35. A) Metrecal

36. C) The Mainframe Computer

37. B) The Picture Phone

38. B) Diners Club Card

39. C) Futurama

40. D) Time for Beany

41. B) Carhop Supermarket

42. C) The Woof-O-Matic

43. A) Dream House

44. D) Bermuda Shorts

45. B) Ankle Beauty

46. A) Southdale Center

47. B) The Theremin

48. C) Charm Bracelets
49. C) Pre-Sliced Cheese
50. A) Dry Shampoo
51. D) The Color Organ
52. C) The Tabletop Grill
53. B) The Drive-In
54. D) The Hula Hoop
55. D) The Friendly Giant
56. B) Military Surplus Jackets
57. A) The Atomic Vacuum
58. B) The Television Stand
59. B) Wobble Shoes
60. B) The Hollywood Diet

ANSWERS 1960s

1. B) Tie-Dye Shirts
2. B) The Beatles
3. B) Rock 'n' Roll
4. C) Star Trek
5. B) The Flying Car
6. C) The Meal Pill
7. B) The Peace Sign
8. A) Magic Eye Posters
9. C) Pre-Sliced Bread
10. C) The Twist
11. A) Mirrors Everywhere
12. B) X-Ray Glasses
13. B) Glow-in-the-Dark Ties
14. C) Cruising
15. C) The Swim
16. C) The Answering Machine
17. A) Building a Treehouse
18. B) The Flintstones
19. C) The Volkswagen Bus
20. D) Subliminal Records
21. A) DIY Rocket Kits
22. B) Go-Go Boots
23. D) Twinkies

24. B) The Blender
25. D) Drainpipe trousers
26. B) Spirograph
27. A) Woodstock
28. B) The Self-Cleaning Oven
29. A) Tang
30. A) The Jetsons
31. C) Bacon Soda
32. C) Language Labs
33. A) The Inflatable Chair
34. C) Optical Art (Op Art)
35. A) The risk of bedside flooding
36. B) The Invisible Ink Pen
37. A) The Lava Lamp
38. C) The Wham-O Super Ball
39. A) Bell-bottoms
40. C) LEGO Bricks
41. C) The Slide Projector
42. D) Monopoly
43. B) "Little Shop of Horrors"
44. D) Molded Meal Madness
45. D) "Get Smart"
46. C) Paper Dresses
47. A) Twiggy Lashes

48. D) The Yo-Yo
49. B) The Amphicar (car/boat)
50. A) Smokey the Bear
51. C) The Vacuum Tube Transport System
52. A) The Pogo Stick
53. C) The Automatic Egg Cooker
54. A) Mood Rings
55. A) The Electric Typewriter
56. C) Earth Day
57. A) The Stationary Bicycle
58. D) The Barking Dog Alarm
59. A) The Magic 8 Ball
60. D) Aluminum Foil TV Dinners

I'M SORY, DID I ROLL
MY EYES OUT LOUD?

ANSWERS 1970s

1. C) The Afro
2. C) Tab Clear
3. C) Seinfeld
4. B) A UFO
5. B) Pong
6. B) Nixon's Plumbers
7. A) Volkswagen Beetle
8. B) The Atkins Diet
9. A) "Stayin' Alive" by the Bee Gees
10. A) 2.5 pounds
11. B) Louise Brown
12. D) Monty Python
13. A) This was actually said in the '90s by Bill Clinton, trick question!
14. A) Take color photos
15. B) Doctor Who
16. B) Petroleum
17. C) Post-it Notes
18. A) Covering them with black soot
19. A) Aerosol sprays
20. C) The Video Cassette Recorder (VCR)
21. C) Chimpanzees
22. C) Flash cubes
23. A) My Mother the Car

24. D) Sirimavo Bandaranaike
25. B) Disco Rock
26. C) Carrot juice
27. B) As a method to encrypt data.
28. D) Get Smart
29. A) Military communication
30. B) A certificate of ownership
31. C) Prancercise
32. B) A "Face on Mars" formation
33. C) "Blinded by the Light" by Manfred Mann's Earth Band
34. A) Smoking at their desks
35. C) Flammable nylon pajamas
36. B) Live goldfish in tiny bags
37. B) Companionship without the mess
38. A) A stiff wire shaped like a leash
39. B) Rocket mail
40. A) "Public Morals," a comedy about vice squad cops
41. A) Celery
42. B) An entire room
43. B) The "Do Nothing" meditation craze
44. C) Non-stick pans

45. A) Led Zeppelin

46. D) Edible glitter pills for sparkly bodily functions

47. B) Exotic pets

48. D) "Fortunate Son" by Creedence Clearwater Revival

49. C) Playing music

50. A) The synthesizer

51. A) The Partridge Family

52. B) The Rolling Stones with the "Tongue and Lip Design"

53. D) "Stayin' Alive" by the Bee Gees

54. B) Pittsburgh Steelers

55. D) Walt Frazier

56. A) A perfect score in gymnastics

57. C) Roger Maris (Note: Though Maris set the record in 1961, it famously stood through the '70s and beyond, until McGwire and Sosa broke it in the late '90s.)

58. A) Instant replay

59. A) Fidel Castro

60. D) The Electric Slide

ANSWERS 1980s

1. B) The VCR
2. B) Young urban professionals
3. B) Tetris
4. B) The Terminator
5. A) Jazzercise
6. B) Knight Rider
7. C) New Coke
8. D) Aerobic Chic
9. B) Sandra Day O'Connor
10. B) Military Communications
11. C) Clue (Cluedo)
12. A) "Girls Just Want to Have Fun" by Cyndi Lauper
13. D) Columbia
14. D) The graphical user interface (GUI)
15. D) Boris Becker
16. C) A collective of young, up-and-coming actors
17. D) Charlie's Angels
18. A) A teaching tool for mathematics
19. A) Tron
20. A) The Amazon Rainforest

ANSWERS 1980s

21. D) The Macintosh
22. D) Halo
23. A) Aretha Franklin
24. A) Star Wars
25. B) E.T. the Extra-Terrestrial
26. B) Carlos Lopes
27. B) Motorola
28. C) Suits with broad shoulder pads
29. B) Sally Ride
30. C) Gucci
31. B) A computer-generated TV host
32. B) The Breakfast Club
33. D) The Flashdance effect
34. B) Cassette Tapes
35. A) Margaret Thatcher
36. C) New Wave
37. D) All of the above
38. C) The Montreal Protocol
39. B) "We begin bombing in five minutes."
40. B) Jeans
41. D) Parachute pants
42. A) KITT
43. B) Richard Simmons

44. C) Going to the video rental store

45. A) Swatch Watches

46. B) Pepsi

47. C) Footloose

48. B) Cabbage Patch Kids

49. C) Pac-Man

50. C) The Buggles - "Video Killed the Radio Star"

51. C) Dallas

52. A) Fruit Roll-Ups

53. A) The BMX Bike

54. B) The Snow Cone Machine

55. A) Wearing two different colored socks

56. B) Murder Mystery Parties

57. B) ALF

58. A) Safety pins

59. C) Live Aid

60. B) The Walkman

ANSWERS 1990s

1. C) Tamagotchi
2. A) The Discman
3. D) Slip dresses
4. B) Friends
5. A) Crystal Pepsi
6. B) Sonic the Hedgehog
7. C) Twister
8. B) AOL
9. A) The Macarena
10. B) Frosted Flakes
11. A) The Palm Pilot
12. C) Tied around the waist
13. B) Princess the Bear
14. C) Backstreet Boys
15. C) Cassette tape
16. A) Where in the World Is Carmen Sandiego?
17. B) Platform shoes
18. D) Dancing Baby
19. A) Dial-up Modem
20. C) A League of Their Own
21. D) Microsoft Office
22. A) Furby
23. D) Orbitz

24. B) Pokémon Cards

25. C) The Matrix

26. C) The Cha Cha Slide

27. C) Scrunchies

28. B) The fax machine

29. C) Star Trek: The Next Generation

30. B) Honda Civic

31. B) Chicago Bulls

32. C) Seattle, Washington

33. B) Brandi Chastain

34. A) Seinfeld

35. A) The Prodigy

36. A) Kurt Cobain (Nirvana)

37. A) Deep Blue, an IBM computer, defeated world champion Garry Kasparov.

38. D) Wallet chains

39. A) Prince

40. B) Harry Potter

41. B) The Masters

42. C) Steffi Graf

43. C) Jurassic Park

44. D) Bright neon leotards

45. D) The Notorious B.I.G.
46. A) Central Perk
47. C) Saved by the Bell
48. B) Tickle Me Elmo
49. A) Baseball
50. A) Alanis Morissette
51. A) Jumanji
52. B) Sony Discman
53. A) The Simpsons
54. C) Facebook
55. B) Viagra
56. B) "D.A.R.E. to Resist Drugs and Violence"
57. A) Tonya Harding
58. B) CD Writer
59. A) Double Dare
60. C) Mark McGwire

Made in the USA
Middletown, DE
13 December 2024

66840314R00082